REVELATION

CHARTS

REVELATION

CHARTS

J. J. Como

Bold Vision Books
PO Box 2011
Friendswood, Texas 77549

Introduction

If you are interested in end time study, you know there are numerous books, charts, and movies on the subject. Each one gives views and scenarios, and then postulates what possibly could happen in the end of days. The charts provided in this book will aid in your understanding of the events that are to occur shortly on planet earth. For the visual learner, the color enhances each chart and contributes to the easy delineations of the subjects covered. The illustrations are Scripturally sound with the use of word-for-word Bible translations. Included are the artwork showcased in larger images to be viewed and visualized for clarity. Many times students of prophecy want to know the bottom line of a subject and with this book of charts one can get the gist of the material without reading a full account of everything covered in a full manuscript.

The information is these pages are listed in a concise manner so as to view all the material relevant to each subject in one location. It is easy to read and pleasant to the eye. However, the best way to learn the materials, is to use the charts with the *Revelation Study Guide* and the book of *Who is This King of Glory?*—the commentary on the book of Revelation. The desire for each of these books is to help with the understanding of the end time, which is happening in this period of history.

THE GREAT MULTITUDE IS THE CHURCH

From Revelation 7	From other Biblical Prophecies
7:9 – "…from every nation, all tribes, peoples, tongue."	Revelation 5:9 – "… for You (Jesus) were slain and did purchase for God with Your blood from every tribe, tongue, people and nation."
7:9, 14 – "…clothed in white robes, washed and made white in the blood of the Lamb."	Revelation 19:8, 14 – "It was given to her (the Bride) to clothe herself in fine linen, bright and clean; for the fine linen is the righteous acts of the saints. The armies … in heaven, clothed in fine linen, white and clean, were following Him (Jesus) …" Revelation 22:14 – "Blessed are those who wash their robes …"
7:10 – "Salvation belongs (is due) to our God and the Lamb."	Acts 4:12 – "There is salvation in no one else; … no other name … by which we must be saved." Romans 1:16 – "… the gospel for it is the power of God for salvation to everyone who believes." Revelation 1:5, 6 – "… Jesus Christ … who loves us and released us from our sins by His blood, and has made us be a kingdom, priests to his God and Father." I Thessalonians 5:9 – "… God has destined us for … obtaining salvation."
7:15 – "Serve God day and night in His temple."	Revelation 3:12 – "He who overcomes I will make him a pillar in the temple of God and he will not go out from it anymore." (a promise to the churches)
7:16 – "…shall hunger no more or thirst anymore …" (shows partaking of the elements of covenant, bread and drink, and the fulfillment of that covenant)	Psalm 107:9 – The LORD "has satisfied the thirsty soul, and the hungry soul He has filled with what is good." Isaiah 49:10 – "They will not hunger or thirst, neither will the scorching heat or sun strike them down…" John 6:35 – Jesus said 'I am the bread of life; he who comes to Me shall not hunger and he who believes in Me shall never thirst.'"
7:17 – "…shall guide them to springs of the water of life and God shall wipe every tear from their eyes."	Isaiah 25:7-9 – "…He will swallow up death for all time, and the LORD God will wipe tears away from all faces…" Isaiah 49:10 – The LORD "… will lead them and will guide them to springs of water." Revelation 21:4 – "He shall wipe away every tear from their eyes…"

The scriptures in *Revelation 7:9-17* reflect the fulfillment of the New Covenant to believers in heaven by the catching away of the Bride of Christ, so that we may forever be with the Lord, and the Father to dwell among us!

The Rapture of the Church

"Catching Away"
References

In My Father's house are many dwellings, I go to prepare a place for you; I will come again & receive you to Myself, that where I am you may be also (John 14:1-3)

We shall not all sleep, we shall all be changed. In a moment... the trumpet shall sound, dead will be raised imperishable & we will be changed... death is swallowed up in victory (1 Cor. 15:51-54)

Lord will descend from heaven with a shout with the trumpet of God, & the dead in Christ shall rise first. Then those alive & remain shall be caught up together with them in the clouds to meet the Lord in the air... (1 Thess. 4:13-18)

"Catching Away"
Timing Clues

Jesus will deliver us from the Wrath to come (1 Thess. 1:10)

God did not destine the Church for wrath (1 Thess. 5:9)

Church kept from the hour of testing which comes upon the unbelievers (Rev. 3:10)

Day of the Lord (not the Rapture) will not come unless the Restrainer (Dan.12:1) is taken out of the way (2 Thess. 2:6+7)

John saw bad things which take place after the Churches (Rev. chapters 8-18)

Those with Jesus (at His Coming) are the called, chosen, & faithful (Rev. 17:14)

The Bride is dressed in fine linen (Rev.19:8)

Jesus' Army clothed in fine linen (Rev.19:14)

GOD's Feasts of Israel

	Festival of Pesach, 1st Month (Nisan)				Festival of Shavuot, 3rd Month (Sivan)
	Passover	Unleavened Bread	Firstfruits		Pentecost, Feast of Weeks
Israel was a slave in Egypt	Kill the lamb, and put blood on your doorposts. (Ex.12:6+7) 1st Month, 14th Day (Lev.23:5)	Purge out the old leaven (sin symbol) from your houses (Ex.12:15-20) 1st Month, 15th Day for 7 days: Sabbath (Lev.23:6-9)	Wave Offering of the 1st sheave (Harvest Promise) (Ex.23:16+19) 1st Month, 23rd Day (Lev.23:10-14)	Plants grow in Israel	Wave Offering by Priest of 2 Loaves of leavened bread (Fruit of the Harvest) (Ex.34:22 & Deut.16:10) 50 days (7 weeks + 1 day) after Firstfruits (Lev.23:15-21)
Whoever commits sin is a slave to sin. (Jn.8:34)	Christ our Passover has been sacrificed (1 Cor.5:7)	Clean out the old leaven.... let us celebrate the Feast (1 Cor.5:7+8)	Christ has been raised from the dead the firstfruits ... (1 Cor.15:21-23)	Going away so that Comforter can come. (Jn.16:17)	Coming of the Holy Spirit on this Day The Mystery of the Church - Jew & Gentile in One Body (Acts 2:1-43, Eph.3:4-9)

GOD's Feasts of Israel

Festival of Succoth , during the Seventh Month (Tishri)

Feast of Trumpets	Day of Atonement	Feast of Tabernacles
Trumpets blown A Holy Convocation Offer a Burnt Offering (Numbers 29:1-6)	Atonement shall be made to cleanse you of all sin as a Sabbath of Solemn Rest (Leviticus 16:29-31)	Harvest Celebration Memorial of booths in the Wilderness (Leviticus 16:13-16)
Seventh Month, First Day (Leviticus 23:23-25)	Seventh Month, Tenth Day (Leviticus 23:26-32)	Seventh Month, Fifteenth Day (Leviticus 23:33-44)
Jesus gathering His Bride (the Church) to Himself as a result of the Rapture (1 Corinthians 15:51+52) (1 Thessalonians 4:16+17)	Israel will repent & accept Jesus as Messiah & faithfully follow Him (Zechariah 14:3-11) (Romans 11:25-29)	Families will come to Jerusalem to celebrate this Feast with Jesus as King (Zechariah 14:16-19)

The Revelation Of Jesus Christ

The Seven Seals

WHITE HORSE:
Rider goes out conquering and to conquer: possibly Satan's evil kingdom of Islam

RED HORSE:
Rider granted to take peace from the earth: possibly war

BLACK HORSE:
Rider had pair of scales in hand: possibly famine

ASHEN HORSE:
Rider Death & Hades following granted to kill 1/4 of the earth with sword, famine, sickness, and wild beasts

SOULS UNDER ALTAR:
Souls killed for testimony of God in Heaven

GREAT EARTHQUAKE:
Sun become black and moon red, stars of the sky fall to the earth, 144,000 Jews sealed, Great multitude in heaven

SILENCE IN HEAVEN:
After half hour, angel takes censer with incense & prayers of saints and throws it to the earth; seven angels prepare to sound seven trumpets

All seven Seals will have been broken by the Lamb to expose the prophesies written on the inside and back side of the scroll. These prophecies cannot occur until all the seals are broken to open the scroll. (Matt.24:33, Mark 13:29, Luke 21:31)

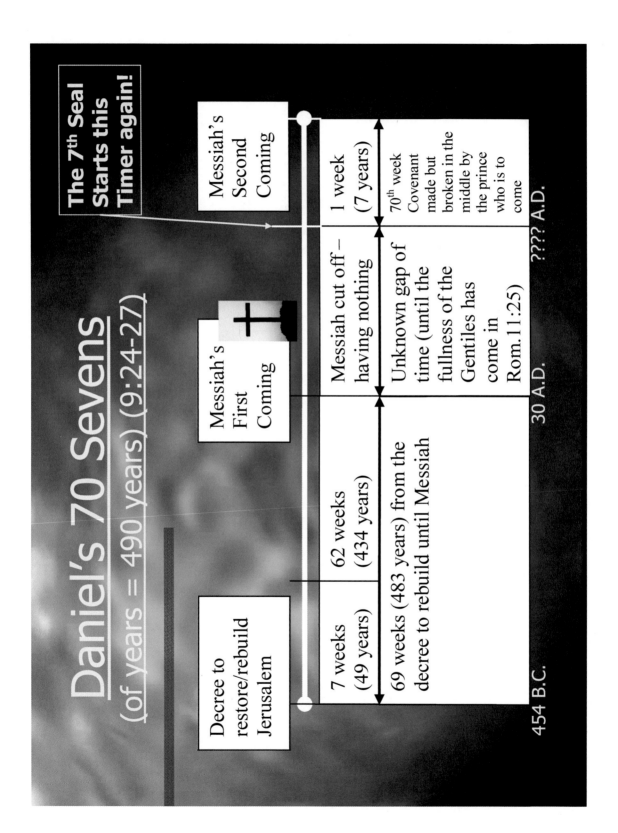

The Day of the LORD

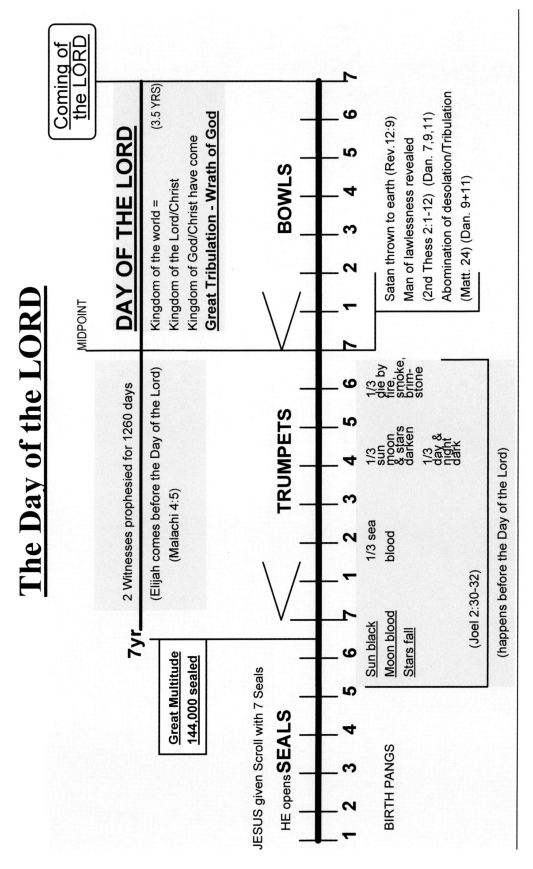

Coming of the LORD

DAY OF THE LORD

(3.5 YRS)

Kingdom of the world =
Kingdom of the Lord/Christ
Kingdom of God/Christ have come
Great Tribulation - Wrath of God

MIDPOINT

BOWLS

7   1   2   3   4   5   6   7

Satan thrown to earth (Rev.12:9)
Man of lawlessness revealed
(2nd Thess 2:1-12) (Dan. 7,9,11)
Abomination of desolation/Tribulation
(Matt. 24) (Dan. 9+11)

7yr

2 Witnesses prophesied for 1260 days

(Elijah comes before the Day of the Lord)
(Malachi 4:5)

TRUMPETS

7   1   2   3   4   5   6

1/3 sea
blood

1/3 sun moon & stars darken

1/3 day & night dark

1/3 die by fire, smoke, brim- stone

(Joel 2:30-32)

(happens before the Day of the Lord)

Great Multitude
144,000 sealed

SEALS

1   2   3   4   5   6   7

JESUS given Scroll with 7 Seals

HE opens **SEALS**

BIRTH PANGS

Sun black
Moon blood
Stars fall

(happens before the Day of the Lord)

Prophetic Overview of Daniel

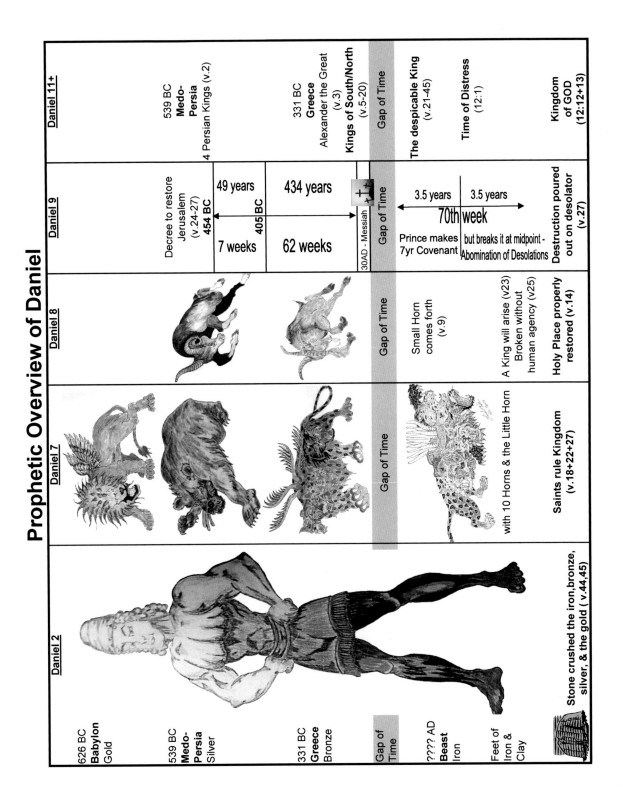

Daniel 2

626 BC
Babylon
Gold

539 BC
Medo-Persia
Silver

331 BC
Greece
Bronze

Gap of Time

???? AD
Beast
Iron

Feet of
Iron &
Clay

Stone crushed the iron, bronze, silver, & the gold (v.44,45)

Daniel 7

Gap of Time

Saints rule Kingdom
(v.18+22+27)

with 10 Horns & the Little Horn

Daniel 8

Gap of Time

Small Horn
comes forth
(v.9)

A King will arise (v23)
Broken without
human agency (v25)

Holy Place properly
restored (v.14)

Daniel 9

Decree to restore
Jerusalem
(v.24-27)
454 BC

7 weeks — 49 years — 405 BC

62 weeks — 434 years

30AD – Messiah

Gap of Time

Prince makes
7yr Covenant

70th week
3.5 years | 3.5 years

but breaks it at midpoint -
Abomination of Desolations

Destruction poured
out on desolator
(v.27)

Daniel 11+

539 BC
Medo-Persia
4 Persian Kings (v.2)

331 BC
Greece
Alexander the Great
(v.3)
Kings of South/North
(v.5-20)

Gap of Time

The despicable King
(v.21-45)

Time of Distress
(12:1)

**Kingdom
of GOD**
(12:12+13)

13

4TH BEAST OF DANIEL

CHAPTER 2	CHAPTER 7	CHAPTER 8	CHAPTER 9	CHAPTER 11
-STRONG AS IRON THAT CRUSHES & SHATTERS ALL THINGS	-DREADFUL, TERRIFYING, & EXTREMELY STRONG -HAD LARGE IRON TEETH THAT DEVOURED, TRAMPLED, & CRUSHED THE REMAINING BEASTS	-SMALL HORN CAUSED SOME OF HOSTS & STARS TO FALL TO THE EARTH & TRAMPLED THEM DOWN	-THE PRINCE & HIS PEOPLE WILL DESTROY THE CITY & SANCTUARY, THERE WILL BE WAR	-KING, A DESPICABLE PERSON WILL COME IN TIME OF TRANQUILITY & SEIZE KINGDOM BY INTRIGUE -OVERFLOWING FORCES SHATTERED INCLUDING THE PRINCE OF THE COVENANT
-FEET & TOES PARTLY OF CLAY & IRON	-ANOTHER SMALL HORN CAME UP AMONG THEM & 3 WERE PLUCKED OUT UTTERING GREAT BOASTS	-SMALL HORN MAGNIFIED ITSELF TO BE EQUAL WITH COMMANDER OF THE HOST	-PRINCE WILL MAKE A FIRM COVENANT FOR 7 YEARS	-AN ALLIANCE MADE WITH HIM, HE PRACTICES DECEPTION & GAINS POWER WITH SMALL FORCE OF PEOPLE
-WILL BE A DIVIDED KINGDOM WITH TOUGHNESS OF IRON & COMMON CLAY	-BEAST WAS SLAIN & BODY DESTROYED & GIVEN TO BURNING FIRE	-SMALL HORN REMOVED REGULAR SACRIFICE & SANCTUARY THROWN DOWN	-IN THE MIDDLE OF THE 7 YEARS HE WILL PUT A STOP TO SACRIFICE & GRAIN OFFERING	-HE WILL ENTER THE RICHEST PARTS OF REALM TO PLUNDER -HE WILL ACCOMPLISH WHAT HIS FATHERS NEVER DID
-KINGDOM: SOME STRONG & PART BRITTLE	-SMALL HORN WAS WAGING WAR WITH THE SAINTS & OVERPOWERING THEM	-HOST GIVEN OVER TO SMALL HORN ON ACCOUNT OF TRANSGRESSION	-THE PRINCE WILL MAKE DESOLATE ON THE WING OF ABOMINATIONS	-HE WILL DISTRIBUTE PLUNDER, BOOTY & POSSESSIONS AMONG HIS FOLLOWERS -HE WILL DEVISE SCHEMES AGAINST STRONGHOLDS
-WILL COMBINE IN THE SEED OF MEN	-4TH KINGDOM ON EARTH WILL DEVOUR TREAD DOWN & CRUSH WHOLE EARTH	-SMALL HORN INSOLENT & SKILLED IN INTRIGUE -HIS POWER WILL BE MIGHTY		-PRINCE GOES TO WAR WITH THE SOUTH & RETURNS WITH MUCH PLUNDER -HIS HEART IS SET AGAINST THE HOLY COVENANT TO TAKE ACTION
-THEY WILL NOT ADHERE TOGETHER -IN THE DAYS OF THESE KINGS (TOES) GOD WILL SET UP A KINGDOM NEVER TO BE	-SMALL HORN WILL SPEAK OUT AGAINST MOST HIGH & WEAR DOWN THE SAINTS FOR 3½ YEARS	-HE WILL DESTROY EXTRAORDINARILY, MEN & SAINTS -HE WILL CAUSE DECEIT TO SUCCEED		-HE SHOWS REGARD FOR THOSE WHO FORSAKE THE HOLY COVENANT -HE SETS UP ABOMINATION OF DESOLATION & DOES AWAY WITH REGULAR SACRIFICE
-DESTROYED, PUTTING AN END TO ALL THESE KINGDOMS		-HE WILL MAGNIFY HIMSELF -HE WILL OPPOSE THE PRINCE OF PRINCES -HE WILL BE BROKEN WITHOUT HUMAN AGENCY		-HE WILL PROSPER UNTIL THE INDIGNATION IS FINISHED WHICH WAS DECREED -KING DOES AS HE PLEASES, EXALTING & MAGNIFYING HIMSELF ABOVE EVERY GOD, & SPEAKS EXTRAORDINARY THINGS AGAINST GOD

OTHER BEAST REFERENCES

The King - Small Horn

Daniel 8	Daniel 11:21-34	Daniel 11:35-45
4 more horns came up in previous horn's place	despicable person will arise	the end will come at the appointed time (last 3.5 yrs.)
* out of one of them came a small horn	* will come with tranquility	
	* will seize power by intrigue	King will do as he pleases
the small Horn	* overflowing forces will be flooded away &	* exalts & magnifies self above every god
* grew exceedingly great to the south, east, &	shattered	* speaks monstrous thing against the God of gods
beautiful land (Israel)	* will practice deception after an alliance with the	* will prosper until the indignation is finished
* trampled down some of the host of heaven	prince of the covenant	* will show no regard for the god of his fathers
* magnified himself to be equal with the	* will gain power with a small force of people	* will honor a god of fortresses with treasures
Commander of the host (Jesus)	* will enter the richest part of the realm to	* will take action against the strongest of
* removed the regular sacrifice (in the Temple)	distribute the plunder & possessions	fortresses
* sanctuary (Temple) thrown down	* will be destroyed by those who eat his choice	* will give honor to those who acknowledge him
* host given over to him on account of	food	* will cause them to rule over the many
transgression	* will be set against the holy covenant & will take	* will parcel out land
	action & then return to his land	
in the latter period of their rule, a King shall arise		At the end time
* insolent & skilled in intrigue	At the appointed time, he	* king of the South will collide with him
* will be mighty, not of his own power	* will return & will become enraged at the holy	* king of the North will storm against him
* will destroy to an extraordinary degree	covenant & take action	* many countries will fall
* will prosper & perform	* will show regard for those who forsake the holy	* the land of Egypt also
* will destroy mighty men & the holy people	covenant	* will enter Israel
* will cause deceit to succeed by influence thru	* will arise & desecrate the sanctuary fortress &	* will pitch his tents between the seas & the
shrewdness	do away with the regular sacrifice (in Temple)	beautiful Holy Mountain
* will magnify himself in heart	* will set up the Abomination of Desolation	
* will destroy many at ease	* will turn by smooth words to godlessness those	The King will come to his end & no one will help him
* will oppose the Prince	who act wickedly toward the holy covenant	
* will be broken without human agency		
	Some Jews will take action	

15

OTHER BEAST REFERENCES

The Abomination of Desolation	Man of Lawlessness	The Beast
Matthew 24	II Thessalonians 2	Revelation 13
Many will come in My Name saying "I am the Christ" and mislead many	The Day of the Lord will not come unless the apostasy comes first	Beast comes up out of the sea * had 10 horns with 10 diadems & 7 heads with * body like a leopard
Wars, famines, earthquakes are merely the beginning of birth pangs	Then the Man of Lawlessness is revealed * called son of destruction	* feet like a bear * mouth like a lion * the Dragon gave the beast power & throne &
Then some tribulation & lawlessness * the one who endures to the end will be saved	* opposed & exalts self above every god or object of worship	great authority * had an apparent fatal wound on one of its heads
When you see the Abomination of Desolation standing in the Holy Place * let those in Judea flee	* takes seat in Temple of God displaying self as being God * activity in accordance with Satan	that healed * whole earth amazed & followed * was given a mouth speaking arrogant words &
Then great tribulation such as not occurred since the Creation until now	* performs with powerful signs & wonders * performs with all deception of wickedness	blasphemies * given authority to act for 42 months
* unless those days had been cut short no life would have been saved * days will be cut short for the elect		* blasphemes God, His Name & His people * was permitted to make war with the saints & overcome them
Many false Christ's & false prophets will arise to mislead even the elect		* was given authority over every tribe, people, tongue, & nation * all who dwell on the earth will worship him,
Immediately after the Tribulation * the sun & moon will be darkened * the stars will fall from the sky * powers of the heavens will be shaken		whose names are not in the Lamb's book of life
Then the Son of Man will appear * all the tribes of the earth will mourn * He will send angels to gather His Elect		

16

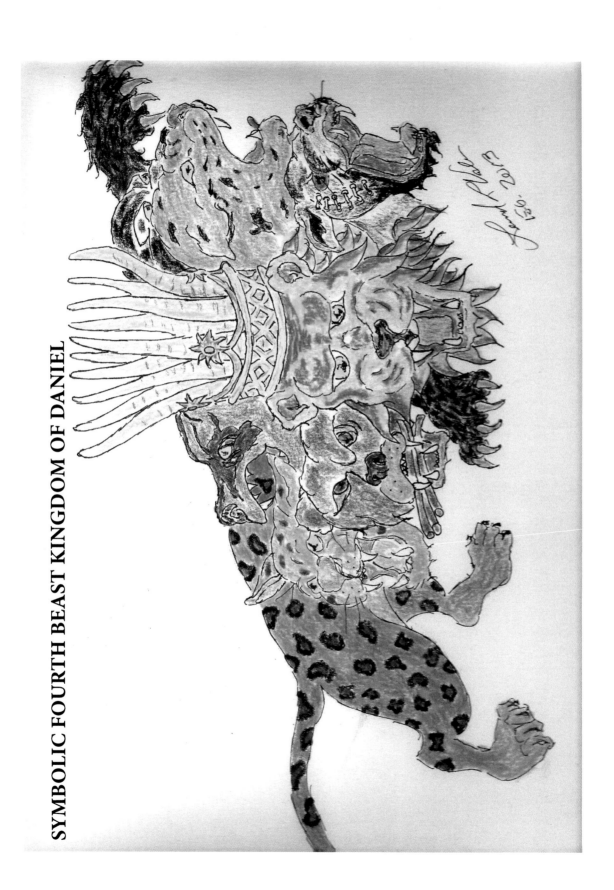

SYMBOLIC FOURTH BEAST KINGDOM OF DANIEL

Ancient Kingdoms

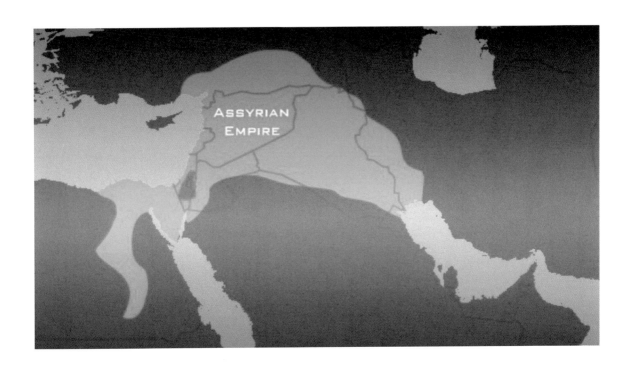

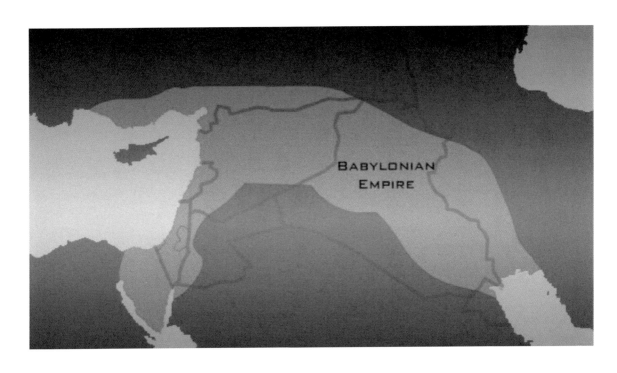

Ancient Kingdoms

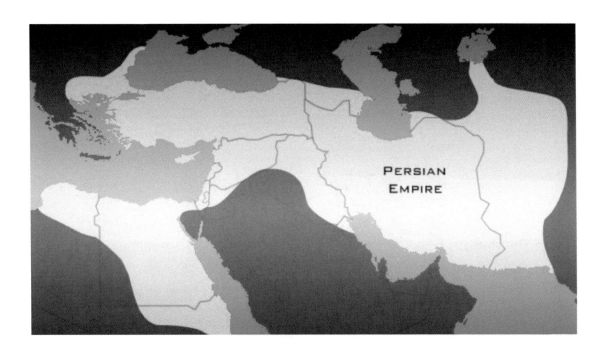

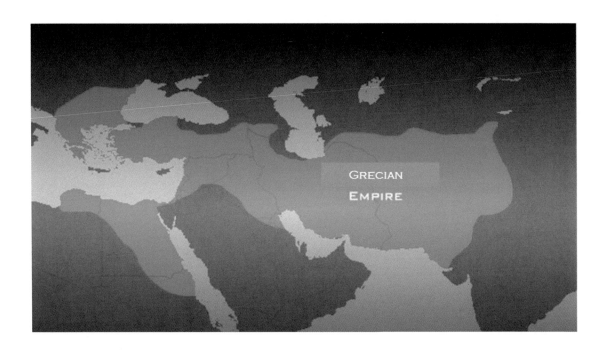

SYMBOLIC KINGDOM OF BABYLON

SYMBOLIC MEDO-PERSIAN KINGDOM

SYMBOLIC MEDO-PERSIAN KINGDOM

SYMBOLIC GREEK KINGDOM

SYMBOLIC GREEK KINGDOM

BEAST KINGDOMS

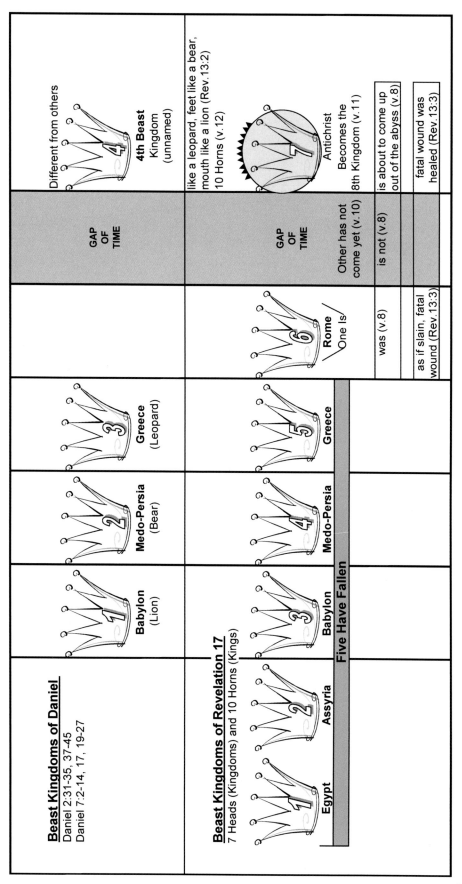

Beast Kingdoms of Daniel
Daniel 2:31-35, 37-45
Daniel 7:2-14, 17, 19-27

Babylon (Lion) **1**	Medo-Persia (Bear) **2**	Greece (Leopard) **3**		GAP OF TIME	Different from others **4** 4th Beast Kingdom (unnamed)

Beast Kingdoms of Revelation 17
7 Heads (Kingdoms) and 10 Horns (Kings)

Egypt **1** Assyria **2** | Babylon **3** | Medo-Persia **4** | Greece **5** | Rome **6** One Is | GAP OF TIME Other has not come yet (v.10) | like a leopard, feet like a bear, mouth like a lion (Rev.13:2) 10 Horns (v.12) **7** Antichrist Becomes the 8th Kingdom (v.11)

Five Have Fallen

was (v.8) | is not (v.8) | is about to come up out of the abyss (v.8)

as if slain, fatal wound (Rev.13:3) | | fatal wound was healed (Rev.13:3)

The Mark of
the Beast

Wallid Shoebat, a former PLO and now a Christian evangelist, said that when he saw the Greek symbol that is translated as "666" in the Bible, he immediately read it as the Arabic character "bismallah" which means "in the name of Allah."

Below are photos of Greek symbols translated as "666" from FreeJesus.Net: The gold symbol (bottom and right) is the Arabic for Allah or "in the name of Allah." There is a least one sect of Islam that considers "666" to demonstrate the perfection of the Quran and prove that Mohammed is the prophet of Allah. In the "666" we find both Islam and Allah.

Hinds & Noble - 1897 - Rev. 13:18 Interlinear New Testament

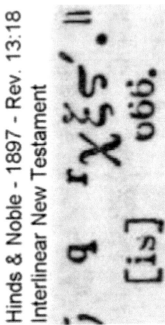

Codex Vaticanus - A.D. 350

Comparison/Parallels of Matthew 24 and Luke 21

Matthew 24	Luke 21
VS. 2: Jesus says, "Do you see these things? Not one stone shall be left upon another which will not be torn down."	VS. 6: Jesus says, "As for these things you are looking at; the days will come in which there will not be left one stone upon another which will not be torn down."
VS. 3: Disciples ask, "When will these things be and what will be the sign...?"	VS. 7: Disciples questioned, "when will these things be? And what will be the sign...?"
VS. 4-5: Jesus answered, "See to it that no one misleads you. For many will come in My name...."	VS. 8: He said, " See to it that you be not mislead, for many will come in My name...."
VS. 6: And you will be hearing of wars and rumors of wars; see that you are not frightened, for those things must take place, but that is not yet the end.	VS. 9: And when you hear of wars and disturbances, do not be terrified: for these things must take place first, but the end does not follow immediately.
VS. 7: For nation will rise against nation, and kingdom against kingdom, and in various places there will be famines and earthquakes.	VS. 10-11: Nation will rise against nation, and kingdom against kingdom, and there will be great earthquakes, and in various places plagues and famines, and there will be terrors and great signs from heaven.
VS. 9-10: Then they will deliver you to tribulation, and will kill you and you will be hated by all nations on account of My name.	VS. 16-17: But you will be delivered up...and will put some of you to death and you will be hated by all on account of My name.
VS. 13: But the one who endures to the end he shall be saved.	VS. 19: By your endurance you will gain your lives.
VS. 15-18: When you see the Abomination of Desolation, which was spoken of through Daniel the prophet, standing in the holy place, then let those who are in Judea flee to the mountains: ...let him who is in the field not turn back.	VS. 20-22: When you see Jerusalem, surrounded by armies, then recognize that her desolation is at hand. Then let those who are in Judea flee to the mountains... and let not those who are in the country enter the city.
VS. 19-22: But woe to those who are with child and to those who nurse babes in those days. Then there will be a great tribulation such as has not occurred since the beginning of the world until now nor ever shall.	VS. 23-24: Woe to those who are with child and those who nurse babes in those days; for there will be great distress upon the land and wrath to this people, and they will fall by the edge of the sword.
VS. 29-30: ...the sun will be darkened, and the moon will not give its light, and the stars will fall from the sky, and the powers of the heavens will be shaken... they will see the Son of Man coming on the clouds of the sky with power and great glory.	VS. 25-27: There will be signs in sun, moon and stars, and upon the earth dismay among nations; ...for the powers of the heavens will be shaken. And then they will see the Son of Man coming in a cloud with power and great glory.
VS. 32-35: ...when you see all these things, recognize that He is near, right at the door. Truly, I say to you, this generation will not pass away until all these things take place.	VS. 28-32: But when you see these things begin to take place, straighten up and lift up your heads, because your redemption is drawing near. Truly I say to you, this generation will not pass away until all things take place.

Timing of Events in Matthew 24

Event	Matthew 24:4-14	Matthew 24:15-30
Birth Pangs	4 - see to it none misleads you 5 - many will come in My Name & mislead many 6 - hear of wars / rumors of wars, see that you are not frightened 7 - nation against nation, kingdom against kingdom, famines & earthquakes	
Midpoint of last 7 years		15 - Abomination of Desolation stands in Holy Place 16 - Judeans flee to the mountains
Last 3.5 years	9 - deliver you to tribulation / killed / hated by all nations 10 - many fall away / deliver up / hate one another 11 - many false prophets arise / mislead many 12 - lawlessness increased / peoples love grows cold	21 - great tribulation 24 - false christs/prophets will arise, show great signs/wonders to mislead 28 - where the corpse is, the vultures gather 29 - sun/moon darkened, stars fall, powers of heavens shaken
The End / Coming of the LORD	13 - one who endures to the end will be saved 14 - gospel of the kingdom preached in whole world to all nations, then the end will come	30 - sign of the Son of Man will appear in the sky with power and much glory

Fullness of the Gentiles vs. Times of the Gentiles

Fullness of the Gentiles	Times of the Gentiles
Romans 11:17-18 Some branches broken off/Gentile nations grafted in; Gentiles nations warned not to be arrogant toward branches; root supports; became partakers with them of the rich root of the olive tree.	**Luke 21:20 Setting: Destruction of Jerusalem** **Luke 21:22** Days of vengeance that the things written may be fulfilled.
Romans 11:20 Jews broken off for unbelidf/but Gentile nations stand by faith: don't be conceited, but fear.	**Luke 21:24** Jerusalem will be trampled under foot by the Gentile nations until the "times of the Gentiles" be fufulfilled.
Romans 11:22 God's kindness if Gentile nations continue in faith.	**Revelation 11:2** Court outside the Temple has been given to the nations (Gentiles) to tread underfoot the holy city for 42 months.
Romans 11:25 Mystery = partial hardening to Israel until "the fulness of the Gentile nations has come in."	**Daniel 9:26** the people (Gentile nations) of the prince who is to come will destroy the city and sanctuary, its end will come with a flood.
REFERS TO THE SALVATION OF THE GENTILES	**REFERS TO THE GENTILE POLITICAL AND/OR MILITARY DOMINATION OF JERUSALEM AND GOD'S PEOPLE**
THESE SUBJECTS ARE NOT THE SAME	

The Revelation Of Jesus Christ

THE SEVEN TRUMPETS

1 HAIL AND FIRE WITH BLOOD THROWN TO EARTH, 1/3 OF EARTH AND OF TREES BURNED UP, ALL OF GRASS BURNED UP

2 SOMETHING THROWN INTO SEA, 1/3 SEA BECAME BLOOD, 1/3 SEA CREATURES DIE, 1/3 SHIPS DESTROYED

3 GREAT STAR FALLS FROM HEAVEN BURNING, 1/3 RIVERS AND SPRINGS BECOME BITTER (WORMWOOD), MANY MEN DIED FROM BITTER WATERS

4 1/3 SUN, MOON, AND STARS BECAME DARKENED

5 LOCUSTS COME FROM ABYSS TO TORMENT MEN FOR 5 MONTHS: **1ST WOE**

6 FOUR ANGELS RELEASED FROM THE EUPHRATES RIVER TO KILL 1/3 OF MANKIND BY FIRE, SMOKE, AND BRIMSTONE; TWO WITNESSES KILLED IN JERUSALEM BY THE BEAST, 1/10 CITY FALLS, 7,000 KILLED BY EARTHQUAKE: **2ND WOE**

7 MYSTERY OF GOD IS FINISHED (CHURCH); KINGDOM OF THE WORLD BECOMES THE LORD'S AND CHRIST'S, THEY BEGIN TO REIGN; NATIONS ENRAGED, LORD'S WRATH COMES; TIME FOR DEAD TO BE JUDGED AND TO DESTROY THOSE WHO DESTROY THE EARTH; TIME TO REWARD SAINTS,: EARTHQUAKE, GREAT HAILSTORM; SATAN THROWN TO EARTH ENRAGED; ISRAEL THE WOMAN GOES TO WILDERNESS TO BE PROTECTED BY GOD 1260 DAYS (3 1/2 YRS): BEAST GIVEN AUTHORITY FOR 42 MONTHS (3 1/2 YRS) WITH ANOTHER BEAST (FALSE PROPHET); NATIONS TREAD HOLY CITY (JER) FOR 42 MONTHS (3 1/2 YRS); 144,000 JEWS IN HEAVEN WITH LAMB: **3RD WOE**

The Revelation Of Jesus Christ

The Angel Proclamations:

 "Fear God because the hour of judgment has come"

 "Fallen, fallen is Babylon the great, who made the nations drink of the wine of the wrath of God"

 "If anyone worships the beast and his image and receives his mark, he will drink of the wrath of God"

 "Tells the Son of Man to put in the sickle and reap the harvest of the earth for it is ripe"

 "Swung the sickle to earth, gathered the vine clusters and threw them into the winepress of the wrath of God"

 "Tells fifth angel to "put in the sickle and gather the vine clusters of the earth for they are ripe"

The Revelation Of Jesus Christ

<u>The Seven Bowls</u>

 Poured out on the earth, loathsome/malignant sore on the people with the mark of the Beast and worship his image.

 Poured out on the sea, it became blood like a dead man, everything in it died.

 Poured out on the rivers/springs and they became blood.

 Poured out on the sun, it scorched men with fierce heat, men blasphemed God's name and didn't repent.

 Poured out on the Beast's throne and kingdom darkened, they gnawed their tonges with pain and blashemed God and didn't repent.

 Poured out on the Euphrates River, it dried up for the kings of the east and the world, to gather for war of Har-Megedon.

 Poured out on the air, there was lightning/thunder, a great earthquake, the great city was split in three parts, Babylon the great was remembered before God, the cities of the nations fell, every island/mountain not found, 100 lb. hailstones came down and men blasphemed God.

BABYLON

The Great City is the Harlot From Revelation	Unrighteous Israel/Jerusalem = The Harlot From other Biblical Prophecies
The great city was split .... Babylon was remembered before GOD to give her the cup of the wine of His fierce wrath (16:19)	Is.51:17-20 - Arise O Jerusalem! You have drunk from the LORD's hand the cup of His Anger ... These 2 things have befallen you, famine & sword ... full of the wrath of the LORD Ez.43:7+8 - The house of Israel will not again defile My holy Name ... by the abominations they have committed. So I have consumed them in My Anger
Angel says, "Come here & I will show you the judgment of the great harlot who sits on many waters. (17:1)	Hos.4:10-12 - They (Israel) will play the harlot... because they have stopped giving heed to the LORD Is. 1:21 - How the faithful city (Jerusalem) has become a harlot
The woman was clothed in purple, scarlet, & adorned in gold, precious stones pearls, having in her hand a gold cup full of the abominations & unclean things of her immorality. (17:4)	Jer.4:30+31 - O desolate one(Jerusalem)... although you dress in scarlet & decorate yourself with ornaments of gold... your lovers despise you & seek your life Ez.16:10-13 - I (LORD) clothed you (Israel) with embroidered cloth & put sandals on your feet... I adorned you with ornaments,.... & put a beautiful crown on your head. Thus you were adorned with gold & silver
Upon her forehead a name was written a mystery "Babylon the Great, Mother of harlots & of the abominations of the earth (17:5)	Jer.2:20 - I (LORD) broke your (Jerusalem) yoke & tore off your bonds. But you... you have lain as a harlot" Jer.3:1 - But you (Jerusalem) are a harlot with many lovers; yet you turn to Me (LORD)? Jer.3:6 - Have you seen what faithless Israel did? She went up on every high hill... & she was a harlot there Jer.13:27 - As for... the lewdness of your prostitution... I have seen your abominations. Woe to you O Jerusalem Ezek.43:8-9 -They have defiled My holy name by their abominations which they have commited... Let them put away their harlotry...
I saw the woman drunk with the blood of the saints & the witnesses of Jesus (17:6)	Lam.4:12+13 - The Adversary could enter Jerusalem because of the sins of the prophets & priests, who have shed the blood of the righteous in her midst Mat.23:35+36 - upon Israel may fall the guilt of all the righteous blood shed on the earth (Also in Luke 11:47-51)
The 10 horns you saw & the beast will hate the harlot & will make her desolate, naked, & will eat her flesh & burn her up with fire (17:16)	Ezek.16:37-41 - I (LORD) shall gather all your lovers against you (Israel)... & expose your nakedness.... They will burn your houses with fire... Then I will stop you from playing the harlot Ezek.23:22-30 - I (LORD) will arouse your lovers against you(Jerusalem)... they will remove your nose & ears, & your survivors will... be consumed with fire. They will also strip you of your clothes.... They will deal you hatred Is. 1:7 - Your land (Israel) is desolate, your cities are burned with fire... it is a desolation, overthrown by strangers Amos 2:5 - I (LORD) will send fire upon Judah & it will consume the citadels of Jerusalem
For GOD has put it in their hearts to execute His purpose by having a common purpose & by giving their kingdom to the beast until all the Words of GOD be fulfilled (17:17)	Dan.9:24 - Seventy weeks have been decreed for your people & for your holy City (Jerusalem), to finish the transgression, to make an end of sin, to make atonement of iniquity, to bring in everlasting righteousness, to seal up the vision & prophecy, & to annoint a most holy place

BABYLON

The Great City is the Harlot — From Revelation	Unrighteous Israel/Jerusalem = The Harlot — From other Biblical Prophecies
The woman whom you saw is the **Great City** which reigns over the kings of the earth (17:18)	Jer.22:8 - Many nations will pass by this city (Jerusalem) & say "Why has the LORD done thus to this great city?".... because they forsook the covenant of the LORD their GOD & served other gods... Rev.11:8 - Their (2 Witnesses) bodies will lie in the street of the Great City, mystically called Sodom & Egypt, where their Lord was crucified Rev.16:19 - The Great City was split into 3 parts... Babylon the great(city) was remembered before GOD to give her the cup of the wine of His fierce Wrath Rev.18:10,16,18,19,21,24 - other references to the "Great City" Gal.4:24+25 - This is allegorically speaking: these women are 2 covenants, one proceeding from Mt. Sinai bearing children who are to be slaves; she is Hagar. Now this Hagar is Mt. Sinai in Arabia & corresponds to the present Jerusalem, for she is in slavery with her children
I heard another voice from heaven saying "Come out of her (Babs) My people that you may not participate in her sins & may not receive of her plagues (18:4)	Is.48:20 - Go forth from Babylon... proclaim this, send it out to the end of the earth; say "The LORD has redeemed His servant Jacob (Israel) Is.52:11+12 - Depart go out from there (Babylon), touching nothing unclean; go out of the midst of her, purify yourselves... but you will not go out in haste, nor will you go out as fugitives; for the LORD will go before you Zech.2:7 - Ho, Zion! Escape, you who are living with the daughter of Babylon
for her (Babs) sins have piled up as high as heaven & GOD has remembered her iniquities (18:5)	Ezek.21:24+25 - thus says the LORD 'Because you (Israel) have made your iniquity to be remembered... because you have come to remembrance, you will be seized with the hand.' And you, O slain, wicked one, prince of Israel, whose day has come, in the time Hos.4:9 - I (LORD) will punish them (Israel) for their ways & repay them for their deeds
Pay her back even as she has paid & give back to her double according to her deeds; in the cup which she has mixed, mix twice as much for her (18:6)	Is.40:2 - Speak kindly to Jerusalem & call out to her that warfare has ended, that her iniquity has been removed, that she has received of the LORD's hand double for all her sins. Hos.10:10 - When it is My desire, I (LORD) will chasten them (Israel), & the peoples will be gathered against them, when they are bound for their double guilt. Hos.12:2 - The LORD has a dispute with Judah & will punish Israel according to his ways; HE will repay him according to his deeds. Jer.16:18 - I (LORD) will first doubly repay their (Israel) iniquity & sin because they have polluted My land; they have filled My inheritance with the carcasses of their detestable idols & their abominations.
To the degree that she glorified herself & lived sensuously, to the same degree give her torment & mourning; for she says in her heart, I sit as a queen & I am not a widow & will never see mourning (18:7)	Is.47:7+8 - You (Babylon) said, "I shall be a queen forever.... I shall not sit as a widow nor shall I know loss .... Is.54:5-7 - The reproach of your widowhood you will not remember... For the LORD has called you, like a wife forsaken & grieved in spirit... For a brief moment, I forsook you, but with great compassion I will gather you. Jer.3:8 - I (LORD) saw that for all the adulteries (harlotries) of faithless Israel, I had sent her away (divorced) Jer.5:12 - They have... said, 'Not (from) He, for misfortunes will not come on us & we will not see sword or famine Lam.1:1 - How lonely sits the city (Jer.) that was full of people! She has become a widow, who was once great... Ezek.16:32 - You (Jerusalem) adulterous wife, who takes strangers instead of her Husband. Mica.3:11+12 - Her priests instruct for a price... Calamity will not come on us... Jerusalem will become a heap....

BABYLON

The Great City is the Harlot From Revelation	Unrighteous Israel/Jerusalem = The Harlot From other Biblical Prophecies
For this reason, in one day her plagues will come, pestilence, mourning, & famine, & she will be burned up with fire, for the LORD GOD who judges her is strong (18:8)	Jer.19:3-9 - I (LORD) am about to bring calamity against (Jerusalem)... because they have filled this place with the blood of the innocent.... I will make this city a desolation... because of its disasters (plagues) Ezek.7:3+15 - Now the end is upon you(Israel) & I will send my anger against you; I will judge you according to your ways... My wrath is against their multitude... will die by the sword; famine & the plague will consume those in the city... all of them mourning
The merchants of the earth weep & mourn over because no one buys their cargoes anymore... (18:11+12)	Is.2:6-8 - You (LORD) have abandoned Your people, the house of Jacob, because they are filled with the influences from the east... & they strike bargains with the children of foreigners... their land has also been filled with idols...
The light of the lamp will not shine in you any longer, the voice of the bridegroom & bride will not be heard in you any longer... (18:23)	Jer.7:34 - I (LORD) will make to cease from the cities of Judah & from the streets of Jerusalem, the voice of joy & gladness , the voice of the bridegroom & bride, the land will become a ruin. Jer.25:10 - Moreover, I (LORD) will take from them (Israel) the voice of joy & gladness, the voice of the bridegroom & bride, the sound of the millstone & the light of the lamp.
in her was found the blood of the prophets & saints & all who have been slain on the earth. (18:24)	Ezek. 22:3-13 - You (Israel) have become guilty by the blood which you have shed & defiled by your idols which you have made...Slanderous men have been in you for the purpose of shedding of blood... In you, they have taken bribes to shed blood.... Behold then, I (LORD) smite My hand...at the bloodshed which is among you. Ezek.36:18 - Therefore, I (LORD) poured My wrath on them (Israel) for the blood which they had shed on the land, because they had defiled it with their idols. Matt.23:35 - so that upon you (Israel) may fall the guilt of all the righteous blood shed on earth, from the blood of righteous Abel to Zechariah whom you murdered. Luke 11:47-51 - Woe to you! For you build the tombs of the prophets & it was your fathers that killed them...I will send to them prophets & apostles & some of them they will kill & some they will persecute; in order that the Jews will be held accoutable for the blood of all the prophets

Parallels of Treading the Winepress of the Fierce Wrath of God

From Revelation	From other Biblical Prophecies
Revelation 11:2 – " …. has been given to the nations; and they will tread underfoot the holy city (Jerusalem) for 42 months."	**Jeremiah 25:15-16, 18**– "The Lord says 'Take this cup of the wine of wrath… and cause all the nations… to drink it. And they shall drink and stagger and go mad because of the sword that I will send… ' … to make them a ruin, a horror, a hissing, and a curse…" **Jeremiah 25:29** – "I am beginning to work calamity in this city which is called by My name." **Jeremiah 25:30** – "The Lord will roar from on high… against His fold. He will shout like those who tread the grapes…"
Revelation 14:18b-20 – "Put in your sickle and gather … the vine of the earth because her grapes are ripe. And the angel… threw them into the great winepress of the wrath of God. And the winepress was trodden outside the city… for 200 miles."	**Joel 3:12-14** – "Let the nations… come up… I will sit to judge all the surrounding nations. Put in the sickle for the harvest is ripe. Come tread for the winepress is full…" **Isaiah 34:2-3** – "For the Lord's indignation is against all the nations and His wrath against all their armies… He has given them over to slaughter… and the mountains will be drenched with their blood."
	Isaiah 34:6-8 – "The sword of the Lord is filled with blood… For the Lord has a sacrifice in Bozrah and a great slaughter in the land of Edom. Thus, their land will be soaked with blood. For the Lord has a day of vengeance…"
Revelation 19:13 – "He was clothed with a robe dipped in blood and His name is the Word of God."	**Isaiah 63:1-6** – "Who is this who comes from Edom, with His garments of glowing colors from Bozrah…? … Why is your apparel red and your garments like the One who treads in the winepress? I have trodden the wine trough alone… in My anger and trampled them in My wrath: their lifeblood is sprinkled on My garments and I stained all My raiment… I trod down the peoples in My anger and made them drunk in My wrath, and I poured out their lifeblood on the earth." **Habakkuk 3:3-7** – "God comes from Teman and the Holy One from Mt. Paran (Edom). His splendor covers the heavens… His radiance is like the sunlight… Before Him goes pestilence and plague comes after Him. He stood and surveyed the earth; He looked and startled the nations."

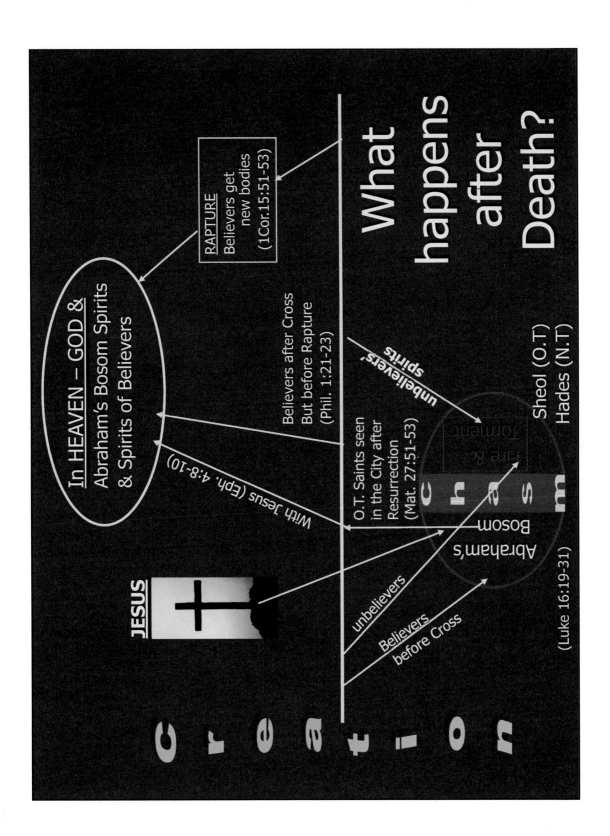

What happens after Death?

RAPTURE
Believers get new bodies
(1Cor.15:51-53)

In HEAVEN – GOD &
Abraham's Bosom Spirits
& Spirits of Believers

Believers after Cross
But before Rapture
(Phil. 1:21-23)

unbelievers' spirits

With Jesus (Eph. 4:8-10)

O.T. Saints seen
in the City after
Resurrection
(Mat. 27:51-53)

Fire & Torment

Abraham's Bosom

c h a s m

Sheol (O.T)
Hades (N.T)

JESUS

unbelievers

Believers before Cross

(Luke 16:19-31)

creation

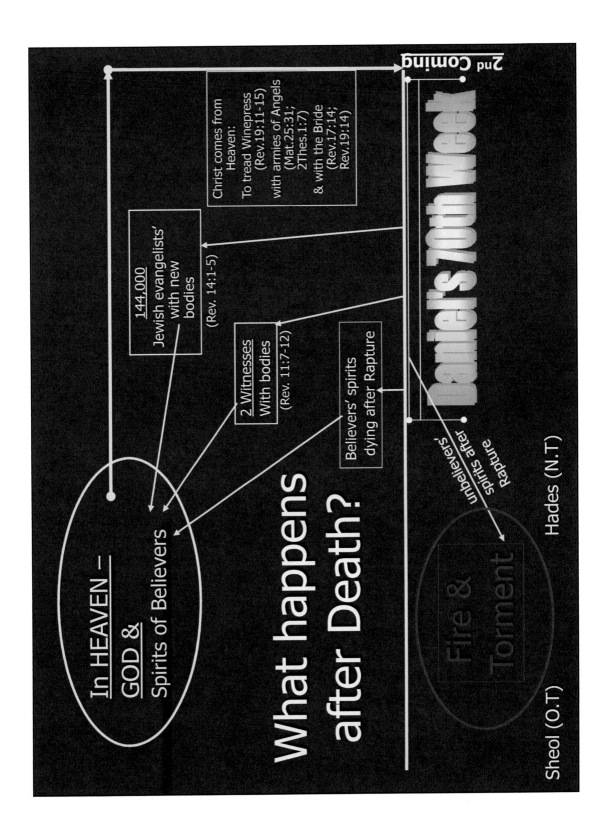

What happens after Death?

In HEAVEN –
GOD &
Spirits of Believers

144,000
Jewish evangelists'
with new
bodies
(Rev. 14:1-5)

2 Witnesses
With bodies
(Rev. 11:7-12)

Believers' spirits
dying after Rapture

Christ comes from
Heaven:
To tread Winepress
(Rev.19:11-15)
with armies of Angels
(Mat.25:31;
2Thes.1:7)
& with the Bride
(Rev.17:14;
Rev.19:14)

2nd Coming

Daniel's 70th Week

unbelievers'
spirits after
Rapture

Fire &
Torment

Sheol (O.T)

Hades (N.T)

What happens after Death?

When Christ returns from Heaven, His Angels gather the Jews from the 4 Winds (Mat.24:31-51). It appears that they do not receive a glorified body, but are gathered to Israel, given His Spirit, & are able to reproduce (Ez.36:22-38)

1st Resurrection (Rev.20:4-6):
- Abraham's Bosom
  (O.T. saints – Dan.12:1+2)
- Souls under the Altar (Rev.6:9-11)
- The Church/Bride (Rev.7:9-17)
- Believing Jews killed after the Rapture
  - These receive imperishable bodies!

1000 year Reign

At the End, Satan released, deceives Nations Battle of Gog & Magog (Rev.20:7-9)

Satan cast into Lake of Fire (Rev.20:10)

Lake of Fire 2nd Death

Beast & False Prophet cast into Lake of Fire (Rev.19:20)

Anyone who dies (Isa.65:1,8-25)

2nd Coming

Sheep enter Kingdom (Mat.25:31-46)

Goat Nations

Satan bound

Beast Armies

Fire & Torment... Sheol Hades

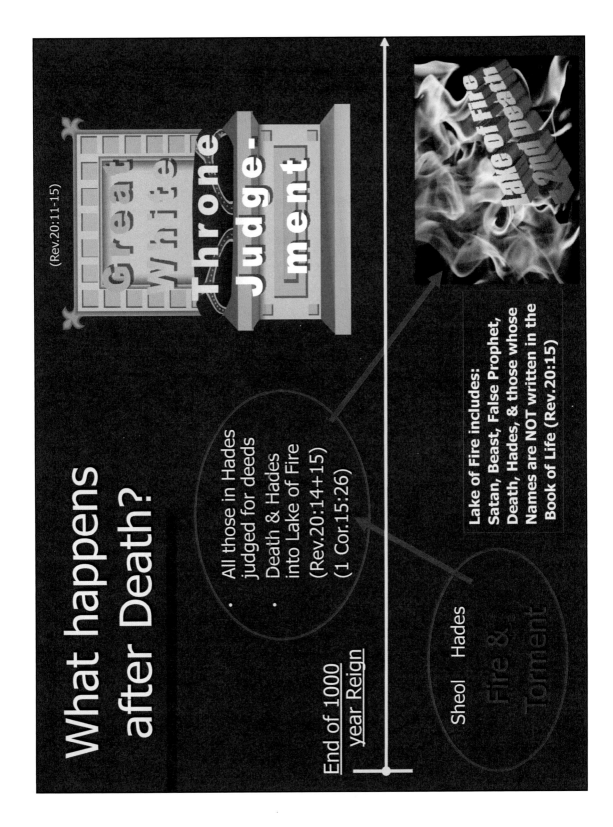

What happens after Death?

(Rev.20:11-15)

Great White Throne Judgement

End of 1000 year Reign

All those in Hades judged for deeds
Death & Hades into Lake of Fire
(Rev.20:14+15)
(1 Cor.15:26)

Sheol   Hades
Fire & Torment

Lake Of Fire
2nd Death

Lake of Fire includes: Satan, Beast, False Prophet, Death, Hades, & those whose Names are NOT written in the Book of Life (Rev.20:15)

What happens after Death?

New Heavens

New Jerusalem

The Bride

New Earth

Sheep Nations & offspring are the nations (Rev.21:24-22:5)

These are in natural bodies that eat leaves of the Tree of Life for healing (Rev.22:2)

ETERNITY!

REVELATION TIMELINE

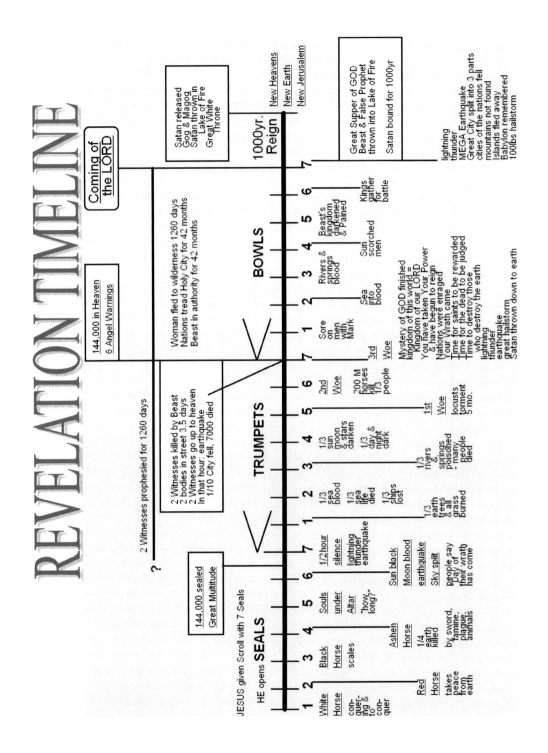

Coming of the LORD

JESUS given Scroll with 7 Seals

HE opens **SEALS**

1	2	3	4	5	6	7
White Horse	Red Horse	Black Horse	Ashen Horse	Souls under Altar	Sun black	1/2 hour silence
con-quer-ing & to conquer	takes peace from earth	scales	1/4 earth killed	"how long?"	Moon blood	lightning thunder earthquake
			by sword, famine, plague, animals		earthquake Sky split people say "Day of their wrath" has come	

144,000 sealed
Great Multitude

TRUMPETS

1	2	3	4	5	6	7
1/3 earth trees & all grass burned	1/3 sea blood 1/3 sea life died 1/3 ships lost	1/3 rivers & springs poisoned - many people died	1/3 sun moon & stars darken 1/3 day & night dark	1st Woe locusts torment 5 mo.	2nd Woe 200 M horses kill 1/3 people	3rd Woe

144,000 in Heaven
6 Angel Warnings

2 Witnesses prophesied for 1260 days

2 Witnesses killed by Beast
2 bodies in street 3.5 days
2 Witnesses go up to heaven
In that hour: earthquake
1/10 City fell, 7000 died

Woman fled to wilderness 1260 days
Nations tread Holy City for 42 months
Beast in authority for 42 months

Mystery of GOD finished
kingdom of this world =
Kingdom of our LORD
You have taken Your Power
& have begun to reign
Nations were enraged
Your Wrath came
Time for saints to be rewarded
Time for the dead to be judged
Time to destroy those
who destroy the earth
lightning
thunder
earthquake
great hailstorm
Satan thrown down to earth

BOWLS

1	2	3	4	5	6	7
Sore on men with Mark	Sea into blood	Rivers & springs blood	Sun scorched men	Beast's kingdom darkened & Pained	Kings gather for battle	

1000yr. Reign

Satan released
Gog & Magog,
Satan thrown in
Lake of Fire
Great White Throne

Great Supper of GOD
Beast & False Prophet
thrown into Lake of Fire

Satan bound for 1000yr

lightning
thunder
MEGA Earthquake
Great City split into 3 parts
cities of the nations fell
mountains not found
Islands fled away
Babylon remembered
100lbs hailstorm

New Heavens
New Earth
New Jerusalem

REVELATION TIMELINE + PROPHECY

Daniel's (9:27) 70th Week (7yrs)

Prince makes covenant for 1 week
2 Witnesses prophesied for 1260 days

Beginning of birth pangs ?

JESUS given Scroll with 7 Seals

Coming of the LORD

Jesus judges the nations
Saints reign for 1000 yrs

144,000 in Heaven
6 Angel Warnings

Woman fled to wilderness 1260 days
Nations tread Holy City for 42 months
Beast in authority for 42 months

GREAT TRIBULATION
DAY OF THE LORD
WRATH OF GOD

2 Witnesses killed by Beast
2 bodies in street 3.5 days
2 Witnesses go up to heaven
In that hour: earthquake
1/10 City fell. 7000 died

144,000 sealed
Great Multitude

SEALS

HE opens SEALS

1 — White Horse — conquering & to conquer
2 — Red Horse — takes peace from earth
3 — Black Horse — scales
4 — Ashen Horse — 1/4 earth killed by sword, famine, plague, animals
5 — Souls under Altar "how long?"
6 — Sun black, Moon blood, earthquake, Sky split, people say Day of their wrath has come
7 — 1/2 hour silence, lightning thunder earthquake

TRUMPETS

1 — 1/3 earth trees & all grass burned
2 — 1/3 sea blood, 1/3 sea life died, 1/3 ships lost
3 — 1/3 rivers & springs poisoned - many people died
4 — 1/3 sun moon & stars darken, 1/3 day & night dark
5 — 1st Woe, locusts torment 5 mo.
6 — 2nd Woe, 200 M horses kill 1/3 people
7 — 3rd Woe

Mystery of GOD finished
kingdom of this world =
  Kingdom of our LORD
You have taken Your Power
  & have begun to reign
Nations were enraged
Your Wrath came
Time for saints to be rewarded
Time for the dead to be judged
Time to destroy those
  who destroy the earth
lightning
thunder
earthquake
great hailstorm
Satan thrown down to earth

Abomination of Desolation
Prince who is to come breaks covenant
King speaks out against the Most High
Man of lawlessness is revealed

BOWLS

1 — Sore on men with Mark
2 — Sea into blood
3 — Rivers & springs blood
4 — Sun scorched men
5 — Beast's kingdom darkened & Pained
6 — Kings gather for battle
7 —

1000yr. Reign

New Heavens
New Earth
New Jerusalem

Satan released
Gog & Magog
Satan thrown in
  Lake of Fire
Great White
  Throne

lightning
thunder
MEGA Earthquake
Great City split into 3 parts
cities of the nations fell
mountains not found
Islands fled away
Babylon remembered
100lbs hailstorm

Great Supper of GOD
Beast & False Prophet
thrown into Lake of Fire

Satan bound for 1000yr

43

Made in the USA
Middletown, DE
08 May 2020

94321202R00027